BEHIND THE TEACHER'S DESK

A Dynamic Resource for Educators

Marjorie Weber Fortney

TEACH Services, Inc.
P U B L I S H I N G
www.TEACHServices.com • (800) 367-1844

World rights reserved. This book or any portion thereof may not be copied or reproduced in any form or manner whatever, except as provided by law, without the written permission of the publisher, except by a reviewer who may quote brief passages in a review.

The author assumes full responsibility for the accuracy of all facts and quotations as cited in this book. The opinions expressed in this book are the author's personal views and interpretations, and do not necessarily reflect those of the publisher.

This book is provided with the understanding that the publisher is not engaged in giving spiritual, legal, medical, or other professional advice. If authoritative advice is needed, the reader should seek the counsel of a competent professional.

Copyright © 2024 Marjorie Weber Fortney
Copyright © 2024 TEACH Services, Inc.
ISBN-13: 978-1-4796-1774-6 (Paperback)
ISBN-13: 978-1-4796-1775-3 (ePub)
Library of Congress Control Number: 2024916460

Scripture quotations marked KJV are taken from the King James Version®. No Copyright Information Available.

Scripture quotations marked CJB are taken from the Complete Jewish Bible®. Copyright © 1988 by David H. Stern.

Scripture quotations marked CWB are taken from the Clear Word Bible®. Copyright © 1994 by Jack J. Blanco.

Scripture quotations marked NIV are taken from the New International Bible®. Copyright © **1973, 1978, 1984, 2011 by Biblica, Inc.**®.

Scripture quotations marked NKJV are taken from the New King James Version®. Copyright © 1982 by Thomas Nelson.

Scripture quotations marked RSV are taken from the Revised Standard Version®. Copyright © 1946, 1952, and 1971 by the Division of Christian Education of the National Council of the Churches of Christ in the United States of America.

Scripture quotations marked TPT are taken from The Passion Translation®. Copyright © 2020 by Passion & Fire Ministries, Inc.

Published by

www.TEACHServices.com • (800) 367-1844

DEDICATION

Dedicated to my God, my sweet family, and all the wonderful teachers I have worked with over the years.

TABLE OF CONTENTS

Dedication		iii
Introduction		9
Chapter 1:	Stolen Money	10
Chapter 2:	Missing Signs	12
Chapter 3:	Chaos in the Cafeteria	14
Chapter 4:	Principal's Prayer List	16
Chapter 5:	Lesson Learned	17
Chapter 6:	An Angry Seven Year-Old	18
Chapter 7:	Planned Deception	20
Chapter 8:	Sleep on It	21
Chapter 9:	Sweet Singer	22
Chapter 10:	She Shoots! She Scores!	23
Chapter 11:	Seventy-Two Minutes	25
Chapter 12:	Milk Snake	27
Chapter 13:	Due Process	29
Chapter 14:	Interrupted Plan	30
Chapter 15:	An Angry Parent	31
Chapter 16:	Freedom to Worship	33
Chapter 17:	Follow the Handbook	34
Chapter 18:	The Stolen Key	36
Chapter 19:	A Priestly Visit	38
Chapter 20:	An Unusual Encounter	39

Chapter 21:	It Looks Like a Squirrel	40
Chapter 22:	Out of the Mouth of Babes	42
Chapter 23:	A Gut Feeling	43
Chapter 24:	The Music Connection	44
Chapter 25:	Tears of Abandonment	45
Chapter 26:	Strange Kleenex	46
Chapter 27:	Black and Blue! Ouch!	48
Chapter 28:	Kindergarten Wisdom	49
Chapter 29:	Note Passing	50
Chapter 30:	Student Celebrities	51
Chapter 31:	Lack of Trust	52
Chapter 32:	God is Amazing	53
Chapter 33:	Snake in the Tire	54
Chapter 34:	Deceived	55
Chapter 35:	Birthday Bandits	56
Chapter 36:	Nine-Eleven	57
Chapter 37:	Time Out	58
Chapter 38:	Aptitude Test	59
Chapter 39:	Rescued	60
Chapter 40:	Change	62
Chapter 41:	Unskilled Voyageur	63
Chapter 42:	A Most Unlikely Maestro	64
Chapter 43:	Needing Fuel	65
Chapter 44:	Special Clothes	66
Chapter 45:	Chosen as Principal	67
Chapter 46:	Tough Constituency Meeting	68

Chapter 47:	Intimidation	69
Chapter 48:	Invisible Visitors	70
Chapter 49:	Holy Spirit Time Out	71
Chapter 50:	Two Correct Answers	72
Chapter 51:	Raw Truth	73
Chapter 52:	Hold the Line	74
Chapter 53:	Discernment	75
Chapter 54:	Test Results	76
Chapter 55:	Drugs in School	77
Chapter 56:	A Prayer Room	78
Chapter 57:	Interference	79
Chapter 58:	Light on the Mountain	80
Chapter 59:	Know Your Gift	81
Chapter 60:	Santa Ana Winds	82
Chapter 61:	Early Morning Visitor	83
Chapter 62:	Weakness	84
Chapter 63:	Strange Fear	85
Chapter 64:	Hypocrite in Uniform	87
Chapter 65:	Urgent Versus Important	88
Conclusion		89
Bibliography		90

INTRODUCTION

"Trust in the Lord with all your heart, and lean not on your own understanding" (Proverbs 3:5, NKJV).

"YOU ARE A BORN TEACHER." The words belonged to my Aunt Millie. She had been listening to the lesson I was teaching to the junior class at Vacation Bible School. I took her statement as affirmation of my desire to become a teacher.

A few years later, I found myself standing behind the teacher's desk in a one room schoolhouse in a small Manitoba town. Today, I was not a student, but the new teacher. I was not just new to this school, but new to teaching in any school. In one hour, twenty-two students would arrive, and I would be responsible for the success or failure of not only the first day of school, but probably also the success or failure of my career in education.

> *I was not just new to this school, but new to teaching.*

My greatest challenge would *not* be sharing knowledge, preparing lessons, organizing schedules, or correcting papers. My greatest challenge would be to create an atmosphere of respect, of making good choices, of fairness, and of caring for others.

The years have gone by quickly. Education was my life for thirty-eight years, as a teacher, principal, and education director. I'm hoping these experiences will help teachers, and principals, as they interact with their students, parents, and community. I am sure you will recognize that most of these experiences took place a long time ago, so always remember as you apply the principles brought out in these experiences, to work within the boundaries and culture that is relevant to your school community, but *never* compromise God's principles.

Your greatest asset is a relationship with your Creator. The experiences shared in this book were possible only because of my wonderful Lord and Savior. It was He that granted the strength and wisdom I needed every day. All the credit and glory belong to Him. If He can take a young blue-jean clad farm girl from a poor family and accomplish what I have experienced, He can do the same for anyone who chooses to serve Him.

STOLEN MONEY

"For nothing is hidden that will not be disclosed, nothing is covered up that will not be known and come out into the open" (Luke 8:17, CJB).

I WAS WORKING AS THE vice principal of a K-12 school when the door to my office opened rather quickly. The principal walked in and without hesitation shared his concern. Four hundred and fifty dollars had been stolen out of the jeans pocket of one of our high school students who had left her jeans in an unlocked locker while she was in physical education class.

What should we do? We knew that we had to move quickly because once the lunch bell rang and students swarmed out of their classrooms and into the halls, our chances of finding the money would be pretty slim, especially since the guilty person would have an opportunity to leave the campus. The clock on the wall displayed the time as 11:50 a.m. An immediate lockdown in the gym seemed to be our only hope.

We divided the student body into groups with two staff in each group. We had everyone empty pockets and remove shoes. One young woman was protesting loudly as to the foolishness of this process. I was suspicious that she might be the culprit, so I made sure I was in her group. I watched carefully as she took off her knee-high boots and observed that she put her left foot down very carefully.

Not wanting to expose her in front of the student body, when the girl asked if she could go to the restroom, I made an exception to the lockdown stipulations, and granted her request. I asked the school secretary to follow her into the restroom and ask the student to remove her socks. Sure enough, there was the money. We chose not to press charges, but we did expel her.

Think on these things:
- Some situations demand decisive and immediate action.
- Teamwork is essential.
- Try not to intentionally embarrass others.
- God still loves those who fall into sin.

Notes:

"True education means more than the pursual of a certain course of study" (Education, p. 13).

MISSING SIGNS

"If we acknowledge our sins, then, since he is trustworthy and just, he will forgive them and purify us from all wrong doing" (1 John 1:9, CJB).

THE NEW WING HAD JUST been completed on the high school building. Everything was new and the students were excited with the new computer lab, the new science lab, and the new classrooms. New signs had been placed on all classroom doors. New lockers were installed. It was an exciting time for students and staff.

I had just returned from an eastern city in Canada after a week of administrative meetings and so the vice principal briefed me on the disappointing happenings that had occurred during my absence. The first thing we had to address was the disappearance of all the new signs from the classroom doors.

After our chat, I made my way to the new wing to have a look at the damage. In the hallway one of the high school students was getting some books from his locker. I called him by name and asked if he knew or heard anything that would tell us who might have taken the signs off the classroom doors. He looked up and down the hallway making sure no one else was present. "Mrs. Fortney, you didn't hear this from me, but I saw who did it." I thanked him and assured him that no one would know that he shared this information with me.

I called the student suspect to my office and asked him what he did with the signs that he took from the classroom doors.

He said, "How do you know that I took them?"

"We're not going to have that conversation," I statedly firmly. "I want to know what you did with them."

He then confessed that they were at home in his bedroom. He brought them back and he was responsible to put them back on the doors in the same condition they were before he took them off, even if that meant he needed to hire someone to get the job done correctly.

Think on these things:

- Students are part of the team.
- Give students an opportunity to make it right.
- Keep your word.

Notes:

"It means more than a preparation for the life that now is. It has to do with the whole being, and with the whole period of existence possible to man" (Education, p. 13).

CHAOS IN THE CAFETERIA

"Boast not thyself of tomorrow; for thou knowest not what a day may bring forth" (Proverbs 27:1, KJV).

IT WAS MY FIRST YEAR as principal at a K-12 academy. Staff morale was low and expectations for the student body lacked clarity. In addition, there was cheating going on during exams and tests in some classrooms.

Setting boundaries can be as simple as implementing a little structure, and so after consulting with the vice principal and staff, we came up with a system and process to eliminate cheating, and at the same time create an atmosphere of order and organization.

We chose a different color for each grade level in grades nine through twelve. We distributed the colors throughout the room, placing different colors on the empty desks in a pattern that would scramble the grades. We, the faculty, were very pleased with our plan of taping blank colored paper to each desk, and we were all ready for Monday morning when the exams were scheduled to begin.

We were not prepared, however, for the total lack of decorum that the students demonstrated on Monday morning. When the cafeteria doors opened, students literally stampeded into the room, jumping over desks, and behaved in a manner that reminded me of young steers being let out to pasture in the spring.

I am not a yeller, but I YELLED, a loud, clear trumpet blast. It was the students' turn to be shocked that such a loud noise could be made by this petite female. The message came through as though an army sergeant had just given the command to "Get out of this room and get back into the hallway, NOW!"

In the hallway I had a pleasant conversation with the students about their intelligence and that this time as they entered the room, I expected them to use their wonderful brains and enter the room like the ladies and gentlemen I knew they were, and that God created them to be. They willingly complied and we never had a repeat of this particular behavior. Our plan of using colored paper to direct the students to a seating arrangement that made cheating very difficult was completely effective!

Think on these things:

- Be prepared and organized.
- The best laid plans will always be helpful, especially in chaotic situations.
- Restore order immediately.
- Do not lose control, even when you have to yell.
- Organization can help to restore order quickly.

Notes:

"It is the harmonious development of the physical, the mental, and the spiritual powers. It prepares the student for the joy of service in this world and for the higher joy of wider service in the world to come" (Education, p. 13).

PRINCIPAL'S PRAYER LIST

"Pray without ceasing" (1 Thessalonians 5:17, NKJV).

> *A grade twelve student came into my office and with great concern expressed that her name was not on the list.*

ON THE OUTSIDE WALL OF the principal's office, in the entrance area of the school building, I attached a large sheet of poster paper containing the names of all the students attending the academy from kindergarten through twelfth grade. This was the Principal's Prayer List.

One day shortly after I posted the list, a grade twelve student came into my office and with great concern expressed that her name was not on the list. I assured her that it was indeed there, and I went with her into the hallway to show her. I was surprised at how relieved she was to know that her name was on the prayer list. I knew the list was important to me, but it was so touching to see how important it was to the students.

Think on these things:

- Don't judge a book by its cover.
- Pray for your students.
- Let the students know you care.

"In a knowledge of God all true knowledge and real development have their source. Wherever we turn, in the physical, the mental, or the spiritual realm; in whatever we behold, apart from the blight of sin, this knowledge is revealed" (Education, p. 14).

LESSON LEARNED

"But be ye doers of the word, and not hearers only, deceiving your own selves" (James 1:22, KJV).

I WAS SUBBING IN A grade twelve Bible class. The students were of their own accord divided into two groups. One group was chatting away and did not stop when the second bell rang.

I placed myself in front of the group that was sitting quietly, ready for the class to begin. "I guess I will be teaching over here today," I announced to the listening students.

With that said, I taught the lesson to the students who were engaged in listening, while the others continued to talk throughout the entire class period.

At the close of the class, I thanked the attentive students for their participation, and then I addressed the group that had continued to carry on their conversation as though there was nothing else happening in the room. I simply said, "Oh, by the way, you will be marked absent for today's class, and I will be giving your names to the principal." I left the room chuckling to myself.

I was scheduled to teach literature to this same group in the afternoon. As I entered the classroom all conversation stopped. Everyone was sitting quietly, waiting for me to begin the lesson.

Think on these things:
- Cause and effect.
- Let the punishment fit the crime.

"In order to understand what is comprehended in the work of education, we need to consider both the nature of the man and the purpose of God in creating him" (Education, p. 14).

AN ANGRY SEVEN-YEAR-OLD

"Jesus said, 'Let the little children come to me, and do not hinder them, for the kingdom of heaven belongs to such as these' " (Matthew 19:14, NIV).

THE FIRST-GRADE TEACHER CAME TO my office and shared that she was out of ideas as to how to deal with a certain little first grader. He was very disruptive and often demonstrated an angry attitude.

I suggested that she bring him to my office and let me spend some time with him. It didn't take long before we discovered the cause of his trouble. He poured out his little heart in response to the question, "Timmy, (not his real name) what is troubling your heart?"

His parents were getting a divorce. He was sure the divorce was his fault. He was afraid that he would not see his father again. In addition to these two frightening thoughts, he fell prey to all the other scary thoughts that many children experience when a divorce takes place.

I reassured him, or at least attempted to. Then I asked if he would just like some quiet time. I also offered to read him a story. The story idea seemed to interest him.

I suggested that when he felt angry and troubled, he could just let his teacher know he needed to come to my office for a story. (I gave the teacher a heads up.) "Timmy" came two more times, and then I didn't see him for quite a while.

One afternoon, just before the busses left, he came running into my office beaming from ear to ear. "Mrs. Fortney, did you notice? I haven't been to your office for a long time!"

Think on these things:

- Get to the root cause of the behavior.
- Kindness goes a long way.
- Some children are carrying heavy burdens.
- Spend time getting to know your students.

Notes:

"Love, the basis of creation and of redemption, is the basis of true education" (Education, p. 16).

PLANNED DECEPTION

> "Be not deceived; God is not mocked: for whatsoever a man soweth, that shall he also reap" (Galatians 6:7, KJV).

CLASS CHALLENGE WAS THE NEXT big event in the school year, and the students in grades nine through twelve were finalizing their plans to be sure their class won the event!

Several grade twelve students came to my office to have their choreography routine approved. I approved their plans, including music selection, and wished them success.

However, when the time for their particular event arrived, the music was very different, and the class began to demonstrate "dirty dancing", a popular dance of the nineties.

I grabbed the microphone and commanded that the music be shut off immediately, and the students were to sit down.

It was their turn to be shocked as they thought they would get away with their plan. They were informed that they received a zero for that section. Unfortunately, that plan and the resultant zero cost them the Class Challenge. Grade eleven took the trophy.

Think on these things:

- Sometimes consequences need to be immediate and public.
- Deception is never from the Lord.

> **It cannot be gotten for gold, neither shall silver be weighed *for* the price thereof. It cannot be valued with the gold of Ophir, with the precious onyx, or the sapphire. The gold and the crystal cannot equal it: and the exchange of it *shall not be for* jewels of fine gold. No mention shall be made of coral, or of pearls: for the price of wisdom *is* above rubies. (Job 28:15-18, KJV)**

SLEEP ON IT

"Be angry, but don't sin" (Ephesians 4:26, CJB).

I TOOK A GROUP OF grades nine and ten students on a social studies field trip. It was an amazing experience of following the process of a tree from the forest to the final product of lumber.

We had a wonderful day. All went well until we were on the ferry home. Some of the students chose to participate in behavior that was in direct disobedience to the expectations that were given to them for the day. I was not happy with them. In fact, I was somewhat upset!

When we arrived back at the school, I made them sit down with me and the principal to discuss their behavior and the consequences of their actions. Parents were waiting and after at least thirty minutes, the parents were not happy with me. It did not turn out well for either the teacher or the students.

Think on these things.
- When you are upset, sleep on it.
- A good night's rest clears the mind.
- Punishment is different than discipline.

Notes:

SWEET SINGER

"There are friends who pretend to be friends, but there is a friend who sticks closer than a brother" (Proverbs 18:24, RSV).

THE SCHOOL YEAR HAD COME to an end. The students had brought many gifts and placed them on my desk. I was amazed at their kindness and expressions of appreciation.

One dear student in sixth grade, stood beside her desk, and in front of the entire class said, "Teacher, my family cannot afford to buy you a gift, but I have a song I would like to sing for you."

She began to sing the song, "Friends Forever." I was stunned. She had such a beautiful, sweet voice. It was a forever moment in my life.

> *The courage and humility that she demonstrated at that moment was amazing.*

When she was done, I assured her that her song was one of the most beautiful gifts I had ever received. It was such an example of Christlikeness. Her character shone forth, and I am sure that heaven recorded her as she presented her lovely gift to me. The courage and humility that she demonstrated at that moment was amazing. What a lesson that precious student taught me that day!

Think on this thing:

- Unless we become like children…

Notes:

SHE SHOOTS! SHE SCORES!

"There is a time for everything, and a season for every activity under heaven" (Ecclesiastes 3:1, NIV).

AS PRINCIPAL OF THE ACADEMY, I would often take a walk around the school partly to keep myself informed, and partly to let the teachers and students know I was interested in what they were doing.

One day, I heard some activity in the gym, and I was curious because the gym was not usually in use during this particular period.

I found several grade twelve boys playing a little floor hockey. They only had one net set up and they were taking turns trying to score a goal. They informed me that they had just finished a test and the teacher had given them permission to go to the gym. They also informed me that they were not able to score on the goalie.

Well, I said in fun, "Give me a stick and see if I can score a goal. Now, watch that upper left-hand corner," I predicted.

I hit the puck, and it sailed right into the upper left-hand corner of the goal. I was shocked. They were shocked. It must have been an angel helping me out. I earned my hockey jersey!

"Well," said one of the boys, "she said, 'Watch that upper left-hand corner.'" No, I did not take a second shot!

Think on these things.
- Seize the moment.
- Take time for fun with your students.
- God has a sense of humour.

Notes:

"Higher than the highest human thought can reach is God's ideal for His children. Godliness—godlikeness—is the goal to be reached" (Education, p. 18).

SEVENTY-TWO MINUTES

"For the word of God *is* quick, and powerful, and sharper than any two-edged sword, piercing even to the dividing asunder of soul and spirit, and of the joints and marrow, and *is* a discerner of the thoughts and intents of the heart" (Hebrews 4:12, KJV).

TEACHING THE BIBLE TO A class of ninth graders is a challenge for any teacher. Even more daunting was the fact that this class period was seventy-two minutes long! Nevertheless, that was my assignment. This was no ordinary class of ninth graders. They were going to be the lawyers and politicians of their generation, at least that was my opinion.

Thankfully, experience was on my side, and of course, the Lord was on my side too. I decided to divide the time into four periods with different activities in each time period, Bible reading/listening, lesson, discussion, and assignment. The deal was if they focused, and we covered the material for the day, there would be a small break at the end of the class.

Reading the Bible aloud and expecting twenty-five grade nine students to listen quietly was a bit of a stretch. However, I knew that although this was a Christian academy, most of these students didn't read the Bible. I also knew that the Word of God is powerful, and it speaks to the heart.

So, at the beginning of every class period, I sat on my high stool and read from God's word. One day, I was quite shocked, although I did not show my surprise, when one of the most disruptive students raised his hand and asked if he could read the scripture for today. "Absolutely," I said, and I promptly gave up my stool.

There were other students in the following days that asked me if they could read as well. It was heart-warming to see the willing participation by several of the students.

Think on these things:

- Only God knows the heart.
- Don't underestimate God's word.
- Don't underestimate the power of the Holy Spirit.

Notes:

"All that had been lost by yielding to Satan could be regained through Christ" (Education, p. 27).

MILK SNAKE

" 'Behold, I send you out as sheep in the midst of wolves.
Therefore, be wise as serpents and harmless as doves' "
(Matthew 10:16, NKJV).

I WAS TEACHING IN A small one-room church school in Ontario. It was a lovely setting out in the country right next to a tobacco farm. It was early September and one day two of my "cherubs" showed up at the school entrance with a huge five-foot long snake.

"Look Teacher, see what we found." I was somewhat terrified of snakes, but I knew this was a test I had to pass.

"Oh great!" I managed to say with fake enthusiasm, as I began to walk directly toward the student holding up this wriggly creature.

Before I even got there, the grade eight boy turned to the younger boy and said, "Aw, let's go, she's not afraid of snakes."

Whew! If they only knew the relief I felt inside.

Think on these things:
- Don't panic.
- Pray for wisdom.
- Smile.

Notes:

The great principles of education are unchanged. 'They stand fast for ever and ever' (Psalm 111:8); for they are the principles of the character of God. To aid the student in comprehending these principles, and in entering into that relation with Christ which will make them a controlling power in the life, should be the teacher's first effort and his constant aim. (Education, p. 30)

DUE PROCESS

"Moreover, if your brother sins against you, go and tell him his fault between you and him alone. If he hears you, you have gained your brother" (Matthew 18:15, NKJV).

AS EDUCATION DIRECTOR I EXPERIENCED a situation where the pastor criticized the principal in front of the entire board. His words were shameful. My role as Education Director provided me with an opportunity to demonstrate to the pastor and the board a better choice. He was not following the principles given to us in Matthew Chapter 18. This was not a singular occurrence, and I experienced the same situation another time in a different school.

Pastors and principals have tough jobs. They need to support each other. If there are issues, follow due process. As a principal, I appreciated the pastors' visits of encouragement and prayer, but I did not appreciate public shaming or destructive criticism in a public forum.

Think on these things:
- Stick to the issues.
- Follow due process.

Notes:

INTERRUPTED PLAN

"So be as merciful as your heavenly Father is"
(Luke 6:36, CWB)

THE SUBSTITUTE TEACHER FOR THE grade seven and eight classes came to my office to ask if I would supervise the students during lunch as she had to run home and rescue a lasagna out of her oven.

I walked into the classroom and was about to sit down in the chair at the teacher's desk, when several panicked voices called out, "Mrs. Fortney, don't sit down, don't sit down! This is not for you. It is for the substitute teacher. She is mean. She treats us like little kids."

I looked down at the chair seat and saw that it was covered in fresh liquid glue.

We had a conversation about the specific behaviors that the teacher demonstrated that brought the students to this conclusion. I was able to explain to the students that this was an older teacher who had not been in the classroom for many years, and she was simply teaching the way she was trained to teach many years ago.

The two architects of the plan immediately and respectfully cleaned up the mess.

Think on these things:
- A little understanding goes a long way.
- Education is the key.

"The Garden of Eden was a representation of what God desired the whole earth to become, and it was His purpose that, as the human family increased in numbers, they should establish other homes and schools like the one He had given" (Education, p. 22).

AN ANGRY PARENT

"A soft answer turneth away wrath: but grievous words stir up anger" (Proverbs 15:1, KJV).

I WAS STILL IN MY classroom finishing up the day when a single parent mom showed up at my door. Everyone else had gone for the day, including the administrative staff. She needed a punching bag and because I was the only one around, I was it.

I do not remember what her concern was, but she was very angry, to the point of tears, and she unloaded on me.

I listened, and when she was done, I could tell she was somewhat relieved. She apologized for unloading on me since I had nothing to do with the situation.

I assured her it was all ok, and I thought she could use a hug. (This was back in the days when hugs were totally acceptable.) She dried her eyes, and we parted on good terms.

The next day she wrote me a very positive letter thanking me for listening. I still have that letter among my keepsakes.

Think on these things:
- Listen, listen, listen.
- Hear, hear, hear.
- Supply the need.

Notes:

"These schools were intended to serve as a barrier against the wide-spreading corruption, to provide for the mental and spiritual welfare of the youth, and to promote the prosperity of the nation by furnishing it with men qualified to act in the fear of God as leaders and counselors" (Education, p.46).

FREEDOM TO WORSHIP

"Let them praise his name in the dance: let them sing praises unto Him with the timbrel and harp" (Psalm 149:3, KJV).

IT WAS FRIDAY MORNING AND the entire student body had assembled for worship. The students were all standing as we sang some spirited choruses, and one of my students was moving in a rather lively manner to the music.

I totally misjudged his movements, and I tapped him on the shoulder. I suggested that he settle down. What happened next gave me a sick feeling in my stomach. He simply wilted as a beautiful, picked flower. I realized I had made a dreadful mistake.

After worship, I called him aside and apologized, stating that I would never want to interfere with his worship to the Lord. Bless his heart he was very forgiving.

Think on these things:

- Mind your own business.
- Appreciate individual expression.
- Be careful not to judge.

The lesson is for all. None can know what may be God's purpose in His discipline; but all may be certain that faithfulness in little things is the evidence of fitness for greater responsibilities. Every act of life is a revelation of character, and he only who in small duties proves himself 'a workman that needeth not to be ashamed' (2Timothy 2:15) will be honored by God with weightier trusts. (Education, p. 61)

FOLLOW THE HANDBOOK

"A wise son makes a glad father, But a foolish son *is* the grief of his mother" (Proverbs 10:1, NKJV).

THE OFFICE SECRETARY CAME INTO the gym where I was involved in some activity to let me know that an angry parent wanted to speak with me.

The parent was waiting for me with her hands on her hips. Her mouth was in gear as soon as I was within striking distance.

She had enrolled her daughter in first grade knowing very well that the school's handbook detailed the school's "no jewelry" policy. Defiantly, the day before school began, she had her daughter's ears pierced and earring studs inserted. She knew what the handbook said, but she went ahead with the piercing anyway. She was angry with me because she was asked to remove the earring studs.

I stuck to the printed word and suggested that she could take her grievance to the constituency regarding the rule against wearing ear jewelry.

Unfortunately, she chose to remove her daughter.

Perhaps you have a better idea for how this situation could have been handled, and how we could have kept the student in school and, at the same time, earned the mother's respect for our school and its stated policies.

Think on these things:
- Written policies have a purpose.
- Be fair with everyone.

Notes:

God's purpose for the children growing up beside our hearths is wider, deeper, higher, than our restricted vision has comprehended. From the humblest lot those whom He has seen faithful have in time past been called to witness for Him in the world's highest places. And many a lad today, growing up as did Daniel in his Judean home, studying God's word and His works, and learning the lessons of faithful service, will yet stand in legislative assemblies, in halls of justice, or in royal courts, as a witness for the King of kings. (Education, p. 262)

THE STOLEN KEY

"...behold, ye have sinned against the Lord: and be sure your sin will find you out" (Numbers 32:23, KJV).

MANY YEARS AGO, IN SMALL schools, policy dictated that the students and the teacher were responsible for janitorial duties pertaining to the space used for school activities. Sometimes these schools were in the basements of churches and the people responsible for cleaning used the janitorial supplies and the janitorial equipment belonging to those churches. Such was the case for this experience.

One afternoon in this particular school, one of the deacons asked to borrow my keys for the church facility, which included a key for the janitor's closet.

Later, he returned my keys, but when I went to unlock the janitor's closet after school, I noticed my key for the closet was missing.

Since this gentleman was the church janitor, and was still in the building, I went to him and ask if he had removed the key for the janitor's closet off my ring of keys.

"Yes," he said, "the head elder instructed me to do this."

I had a very firm conversation with him, which resulted in my key being returned to my key ring immediately.

Think on these things:

- Communicate.
- Be transparent.
- Speak "truth to power" wisely.

Notes:

"Children should not be forced into a precocious maturity, but as long as possible should retain the freshness and grace of their early years" (Education, p. 107).

A PRIESTLY VISIT

"If any of you lack wisdom, let him ask of God, that giveth to all men liberally, and upbraideth not; and it shall be given him" (James 1:5, KJV).

IT WAS MY FIRST YEAR of teaching. My assignment was in a small one-room multigrade public school in my hometown. There were twenty-two students in grades one through eight, and most of the students came from Catholic homes. The parents of the school were very supportive and were simply good decent people.

One afternoon the local Catholic priest paid a visit and asked me if he could come once a week to hold catechism during the last hour of the school day. That was fine with me. I decided that I would just let the three Protestant children leave early on Fridays. Of course, that meant I could leave early also.

A few years later when I returned to university to get my degree, I discovered that it was actually a law in that province, that if sixty percent of the students were from the Catholic faith, the priest had the right to have time to teach catechism in the school. I was glad that God gave me wisdom and a congenial spirit to agree to the priest's request without any argument.

Think on these things:
- Be kind and cooperative.
- Respect other's rights.
- Build relationships.

"Parents and teachers should seek most earnestly for that wisdom which Jesus is ever ready to give; for they are dealing with human minds at the most interesting and impressible period of their development" (Testimonies for the Church, vol. 6, p.204).

AN UNUSUAL ENCOUNTER

"And Jesus answered and said unto them, 'take heed that no man deceive you' " (Matthew 24:4, KJV)

I WAS THE PRINCIPAL AT a junior academy, and one Sabbath after the church service a gentleman approached me saying, "I have new light I want to share with you."

I responded, "Why are you not speaking to the pastor about this?"

"Because you are a better Christian than the pastor," was his astonishing response.

A big red flag began waving in my mind. Flattery does not come from God. I rejected his offer and his assessment.

> *"You are a better Christian than the pastor," was his astonishing response.*

Think on these things:
- Satan is very subtle.
- Stay in your role.

"The greatest want of the world is the want of men--men who will not be bought or sold, men who in their inmost souls are true and honest, men who do not fear to call sin by its right name, men whose conscience is as true to duty as the needle to the pole, men who will stand for the right though the heavens fall" (Education, p. 57).

IT LOOKS LIKE A SQUIRREL

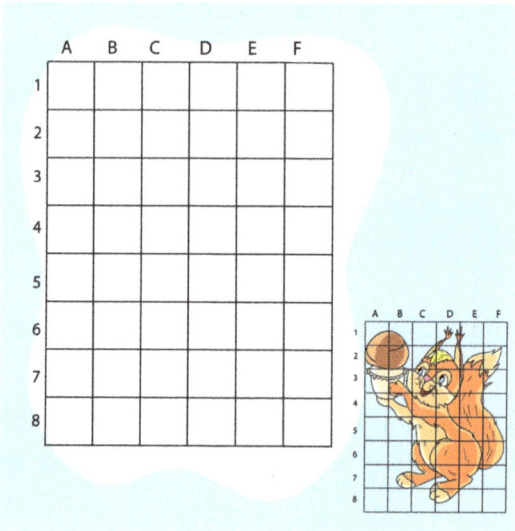

"Then Jesus answering said unto them, 'Go your way, and tell John what things ye have seen and heard; how that the blind see' " (Luke 7:22, KJV)

HOW DO YOU TEACH A blind child in a classroom full of sighted children? That was a situation I had to deal with and what an amazing experience it was.

How does a blind child draw a picture? All the students were using a grid to draw a picture of a squirrel. Those who could see had the advantage of a screen picture of a squirrel drawn on a grid. I gave my blind student a sheet of braille grid paper and verbally gave him the coordinate squares and explained what the lines in each particular square looked like.

The other students were very interested to see what the blind student's art project would look like. When we finished the project, the students gathered around his desk and excitedly exclaimed, "Sean, it looks like a squirrel! It looks like a squirrel!"

Needless to say, Sean was smiling from ear to ear.

Think on these things:
- Nothing is too difficult for God.
- Think outside the box.

Notes:

OUT OF THE MOUTH OF BABES

"But Jesus said, 'Suffer little children, and forbid them not, to come unto me: for of such is the kingdom of heaven' " (Matthew 19:14, KJV).

HER MOTHER WAS A LADY of the night and was not available to guide and support her daughter. The little girl's grandma had stepped into her life and did her best to provide opportunities for her granddaughter that would be valuable to her physical, mental, and psychological well being.

The grandmother registered her at our church school. Learning about Jesus was a new experience for the little girl. One morning as her grandma dropped her off at school, she wished her luck in her test.

She said, "Grandma, when you have Jesus, you don't need luck."

Think on these things.
- Children often understand more that we think.
- Our schools are evangelistic centers.

Notes:

A GUT FEELING

"But let all those that put their trust in thee rejoice: let them ever shout for joy, because thou defendest them: let them also that love thy name be joyful in thee" (Psalm 5:11, KJV).

MANY TIMES, I HAVE RETURNED to the school after eating supper at my home, to complete unfinished school business. One evening I drove up to the school and parked the car. When I opened the car door, I had this strange feeling of being watched. I tried to ignore this feeling, but when I unlocked the door to the school building and entered the school, a strong impression entered my mind to lock the door immediately, which I did.

I entered the classroom and locked the classroom door as well. At that moment there was a banging on the front door. Someone was aggressively trying to open the front door. I do not know who was on the other side of the door, but I believe it was someone who did not have good intentions. I did call my husband who was working close by, but by the time he arrived there was no one to be seen.

God protected me from something, or someone. Some day my guardian angel will fill me in as to who was on the other side of the door.

Think on these things:
- Strong impressions can be from the Lord.
- God has our back.
- Keep a prayer in your heart.

Notes:

THE MUSIC CONNECTION

"Let them praise his name in the dance: let them sing praises unto him with the timbrel and harp" (Psalm 149:3, KJV).

FOR MANY YEARS I TAUGHT the students how to play recorders as part of our music class. One particular year we were able to have soprano, alto, and tenor recorders. The students were fairly musical, so they caught on quickly. They learned to play several hymns and gospel songs.

One young student really benefitted from this musical experience, and he thoroughly enjoyed music. We were invited to play at another school.

He was very excited, and he said, "Mrs. Fortney, we are becoming famous, aren't we?"

This student struggled with his other classes particularly reading, but music was one of his gifts, and the success in music brought much improvement in his other classes. Music encouraged his heart and strengthened his mind.

Think on these things:
- We are created with a musical mind.
- Music is a way of praising God.
- We all have strengths and gifts.

"Even the children should be taught to do little errands of love and mercy for those less fortunate than themselves" (Testimonies for the Church vol. 6, p. 435).

TEARS OF ABANDONMENT

"And God shall wipe all tears from their eyes"
(Revelation 21:4, KJV).

SHE WAS A GRADE NINE student staying with a relative and attending academy. She left the classroom for a washroom break, but as she did not return for a longer than normal period of time, I went to check on her.

She was weeping uncontrollably and, as I inquired of the cause, she sobbed out these words "Why did my mom abandon me? Why did she not want me?"

My heart was broken, and I wept with her.

"I don't know," I responded, but I can only wish I had a daughter like you." We dried our tears and she soon returned to the classroom.

She is now a mother of two, a good mother, and she still keeps in touch with me.

Think on these things.

- Sometimes all we can do is weep with those who weep.
- Gentle words have a powerful influence.
- Christ came to heal the broken hearted.

"We should educate the youth to help the youth; and as they seek to do this work they will gain an experience that will qualify them to become consecrated workers in a larger sphere" (Testimonies vol. 6, p. 115).

STRANGE KLEENEX

> "Behold, what manner of love the Father hath bestowed upon us, that we should be called the sons of God: therefore the world knoweth us not, because it knew him not" (1 John 3:1, KJV).

IT WAS LUNCH HOUR, AND the students were busy eating. I too, was enjoying my lunch. David decided to blow his nose into his orange peel. You can imagine the response he received from the rest of the students. They expressed total disgust with all the sound effects that they could muster.

I had been warned that David would be a real challenge. I asked him to remain inside to visit with me while the others went outside to play.

I asked, "David, do you think Prince Charles would have blown his nose into his orange peel?"

"No," he responded.

"Why not?" I asked.

"Because he is a prince," was David's prompt reply.

"Well, so are you, David," I stated.

"I am?" David asked obviously puzzled.

"Yes, you are!" I assured him as I went on to explain that he was a child of the King of the Universe (now cosmos).

It made such a difference in this little boy's life. I was so glad that we had that conversation as David had a very short life on this earth, but he told his friends he was not afraid to die because he knew Jesus loved him.

Every year at Christmas I hang a special ornament on my Christmas tree that says, "To my favorite teacher, love David."

Think on these things:

- We are all children of the King.
- Life can be short even for the very young.
- Remember who you are teaching.

Notes:

"The Sermon on the Mount is an example of how we are to teach. What pains Christ has taken to make mysteries no longer mysteries, but plain, simple truths! There is in His instruction nothing vague, nothing hard to understand" (Testimonies for the Church vol. 7 p. 269).

BLACK AND BLUE! OUCH!

"And, ye fathers, provoke not your children to wrath: but bring them up in the nurture and admonition of the Lord" (Ephesians 6:4, KJV).

WE WILL CALL HIM JOEY. One day not long after he joined our school he arrived with many black and blue marks on his face, arms, and legs. His story was that his father beat him.

Normally, the social services would be called, and they would take care of the issue. However, because this was a family that immigrated from a country where fathers were allowed to beat their wives and children, and because I had met the father, I called him and asked him to come to my office.

I explained to him that in our country he was not allowed to beat his children or wife and that he could end up in jail. I shared with him that I would be calling social services and asking them to visit his family and explain the laws of our country. He was thankful, and we never saw any more black and blue marks.

Think on these things:
- Use common sense.
- Reach out for resources.

KINDERGARTEN WISDOM

"And thou shalt teach them diligently unto thy children, and shalt talk of them when thou sittest in thine house, and when thou walkest by the way, and when thou liest down, and when thou risest up" (Deuteronomy 6:7, KJV).

THE CHILDREN ENTERED THE SCHOOL after recess and proceeded to their classrooms. I lingered in the hallway for a few minutes enjoying the message and the creativity displayed on a nearby bulletin board. A kindergarten student walked by on his way to the washroom and his comment was, "Mrs. Fortney, aren't you supposed to be in your office now?"

My reply was, "Oh yes, of course, I am heading there right now."

Out of the mouth of babes!

Think on these things:
- Children are so precious.
- Teach them diligently.

Notes:

NOTE PASSING

"Discretion shall preserve thee, understanding shall keep thee" (Proverbs 2:11, KJV).

I WALKED INTO A CLASSROOM full of grade ten students. This was a new school for me, and I was a new teacher to the students. English class is not usually the most liked class by many students, so I did my best to present the lesson in an interesting manner.

As I watched the students passing notes to each other I wasn't sure I was actually reaching the goal of interesting, but I could see that they thought I wasn't aware of what was going on, so I just continued teaching.

At the end of class as I was walking out the door, I turned and said, "It was so kind of you to pass notes to each other instead of talking while I was teaching the lesson." I smiled, and they looked at each other and burst out laughing. It never happened again. They were just testing the new teacher.

> *It never happened again. They were just testing the new teacher.*

Think on these things:
- Keep a sense of humour.
- Keep a step ahead.
- Pop the balloon at the appropriate moment.

Notes:

STUDENT CELEBRITIES

"He that is slow to wrath *is* of great understanding: but *he that is* hasty of spirit exalteth folly" (Proverbs 14:29, KJV).

SUBSTITUTE TEACHING IS ALWAYS A surprise because you never know what to expect; but, when it ends up being a grade eleven class of thirty some students, you can expect anything.

I handed out a lined piece of paper for students to sign their names so they could be marked present. When the paper came back, I saw names like Brian Mulroney, Boy George, etc. The students were waiting for my reaction.

"Well," I said, "had I known there were going to be celebrities here this morning, I would have brought my autograph book."

There was a burst of laughter, and we got on with the class.

Think on this thing:
- Playing the game gives you opportunity to become the captain.

Notes:

LACK OF TRUST

"Fear thou not; for I *am* with thee: be not dismayed; for I *am* thy God: I will strengthen thee; yea, I will help thee; yea, I will uphold thee with the right hand of my righteousness" (Isaiah 41:10, KJV).

I GOT A CALL TO be principal in a certain area, and I said to my husband, "I don't want to go there; they have earthquakes there." So, instead, I accepted a call up in the northern part of the province.

One Sabbath morning, just before we left for church, we experienced a 6.5 magnitude earthquake. It felt like the epicentre was right under our house. The floor was rolling like the waves of the sea and the walls of the house were moving back and forth. The chandelier in the dining room was swinging back and forth so hard I thought it would come crashing to the floor.   My husband and I stood in the doorway trying to decide if we should go outside or just stay put.

Obviously, this was a good lesson for me. God can protect us no matter in what situation we find ourselves. I got the message.

Think on these things:

- Fear not.
- God is real.
- Trust Him.

"In selecting teachers, we should use every precaution, knowing that this is as solemn a matter as the selecting of persons for the ministry" (Testimonies for the Church vol. 6, p. 203).

GOD IS AMAZING

"And have not obeyed the voice of my teachers, nor inclined mine ear to them that instructed me!" (Proverbs 5:13, KJV).

MY FIRST YEAR AS PRINCIPAL of a K-12 school was challenging to say the least. Staff morale was at an all-time low, the spiritual condition of the student body was quite alarming, and as you probably guessed, the academic performance was at the bottom of a scale from 1-10. The high school program needed some major changes.

We were not aware of a report that was being prepared by the Fraser Institute regarding the academic performance of all the high schools in the province. However, when it did come out it was published in all the provincial and local newspapers. Our school did not look good. We were just above 2 on a scale of 1-10.

You can imagine the constituents were not happy, and we all felt quite embarrassed with our score. Yet, it was not at all surprising knowing the current condition of the high school program.

The vice principal and I did our due diligence and God helped us find the problem. Simply put, we established a policy that required each high school student to have a grade of sixty percent or above in order to be allowed to write the provincial exams. This policy applied to all school tests. This really worked. The next report that came out, our school went to almost seven on the scale.

Think on these things:
- God has answers.
- Set standards that are reasonable for all.
- Be consistent.

"Then let the church carry a burden for the lambs of the flock. Let the children be educated and trained to do service for God, for they are the Lord's heritage" (Testimonies for the Church vol. 6, p. 203).

SNAKE IN THE TIRE

"The angel of the Lord encamps all around those who fear Him, And delivers them" (Psalm 34:7, NKJV).

THE STUDENTS WERE ENJOYING LUNCH recess. There were many activities going on here and there. One little girl headed for the big tractor tire. Fortunately, she looked down inside the tire before she jumped inside. There was a baby rattlesnake curled up inside the tire!

We called all the students off the playground and back inside the school. When the huge tractor tire was removed it was discovered that there was a rattlesnake den in the ground. How many times children played there we couldn't count. All tires were removed from off the playground. We all offered a prayer of thanksgiving for God's protection.

Think on these things:
- Angel warriors are on the playground.
- Check your playground for safety.

Notes

DECEIVED

"(According as it is written, God hath given them the spirit of slumber, eyes that they should not see, and ears that they should not hear;) unto this day" (Romans 11:8, KJV).

DESMOND FORD CAUSED QUITE A wave of confusion for many Adventist church members back in the late seventies and early eighties. The head elder of our church became convinced Desmond Ford was correct. Unfortunately, a book that came out around the same time, *The White Lie* by Walter T. Rea, disparaged Ellen White and questioned her authenticity. This elder lost his faith in Adventism and left the church.

Two of his sons were in my classroom. I asked what they thought of all this. They, of course, trusted their father's conclusions, including his decision to leave the church. I expected this response, but I was hoping that there might be a chance they would study for themselves.

Looking back, I can tell you things did not go well. It was heartbreaking to watch. I am soberly reminded how important it is to emphasize the absolute necessity of a personal relationship with Jesus, and to study God's word for ourselves.

Think on these things:
- Age accountability.
- We stand alone in the judgment.
- The truth shall set you free.

"Order is heaven's first law, and every school should in this respect be a model of heaven" (Testimonies for the Church vol. 6, p. 201).

BIRTHDAY BANDITS

"Sweet friendships refresh the soul and awaken our hearts with joy, for good friends are like the anointing oil that yields the fragrant incense of God's presence" (Proverbs 27:9, TPT).

I WAS ENJOYING A FEW moments of quietness in my office after a busy day. The busses were headed home with their treasure of students, and there were no appointments to meet.

Suddenly, two men wearing balaclavas burst into my office, blindfolded me, tied me to my chair and whisked me away. Fortunately, they were my friends.

Down the hall and down the elevator to the lower floor and into the cafeteria we went. They took the blindfold off, and all the staff were cheering and having a good time. It was my birthday! It was time for cake and ice cream.

Precious memories.

Think on these things:

- Enjoy the moment.
- Friendship is priceless.

"When heavenly intelligences see that men are no longer permitted to present the truth, the Spirit of God will come upon the children, and they will do a work in the proclamation of the truth which the older workers cannot do, because their way will be hedged up" (Testimonies for the Church vol. 6, p. 203).

"Our church schools are ordained by God to prepare the children for this great work." ibid

NINE-ELEVEN

"And both these kings' hearts *shall be* to do mischief, and they shall speak lies at one table; but it shall not prosper: for yet the end *shall be* at the time appointed" (Daniel 11:27, KJV).

USUALLY, EVERYONE REMEMBERS WHERE THEY were and what they were doing when the twin towers were destroyed on September 11, 2001. How well I remember that morning. The second bell had rung, and we were about to begin the day when the school board chair walked into the room.

"Have you heard what is going on in United States?" he questioned.

We had not. He proceeded to share with us that the twin towers in New York City were destroyed by passenger airplanes flying directly into the towers.

We turned on the TV and were astonished, amazed, and terrified by the pictures. We realized that many people died as a result of these attacks and that there would be terrible suffering and sorrow for many families.

The students asked if we could go to the church and pray. Certainly, we could do that as the church was next door to the school. Many of the students prayed and together we found comfort in the Lord.

Think on these things:
- The Lord comforts His people.
- Love casts out fear.

TIME OUT

"Ponder the path of thy feet, and let all thy ways be established" (Proverbs 4:26, KJV).

THE SCENE FOR THIS OUTBURST was a mission school in a remote, barren, and desolate location. The student was very angry and it would have been generous to describe the words spewing from her mouth as unkind. I was concerned, wanting this confrontation to have a successful outcome.

I suggested that she sit quietly for a few minutes and when she felt ready to talk, she could let me know. While she was sitting quietly, I was praying that the Holy Spirit would speak to her heart.

In about twenty minutes she said, "I am ready to talk."

I suggested that she knew what she did wrong, and that she also knew how to fix it. She agreed and she took care of the matter.

I used this method many times and the pattern was always the same. They sat quietly and I prayed for the Holy Spirit to calm their heart. It always took about twenty minutes before they were ready to talk.

Think on these things:
- God still speaks.
- Self-discipline can be very productive.

"All things both in heaven and in earth declare that the great law of life is a law of service" (Education, p. 103)

APTITUDE TEST

"For the Lord does not see as man sees; for man looks at the outward appearance, but the Lord looks at the heart" (1 Samuel 16:7, NKJV).

REMEMBER THOSE OLD APTITUDE TESTS? I certainly do. I sat on a chair in the principal's office as he went through the results of my aptitude test.

"What do you plan to do with your life?" he asked me.

Without hesitation I answered, "I am going to be a teacher."

"A teacher, you'll never make a teacher. Maybe a clerk in a store, but not a teacher," he told me.

Well, I couldn't be too upset, since my highest score was in mechanics. I just came straight off the farm so that wasn't very surprising. Somehow, I paid no attention to that interview and just continued with my plans.

Later in the school year, I needed money to purchase some material to complete a sewing project. I had no money, and this class was meeting the extra credit I needed to complete the grade twelve requirements. I went to see the principal about my need.

His unfeeling response was, "I guess you'll have to find a gunny sack somewhere." That was the extent of the conversation.

When I received my first teaching award, that same principal was in the congregation.

Think on these things:
- Words are important.
- God looks on the heart.

RESCUED

*"And it shall come to pass, that before they call,
I will answer; and while they are yet speaking, I will hear"
(Isaiah 65:24, KJV).*

I HAD PLANNED A SHORT vacation to visit my children in Minnesota, but on the way, I took the opportunity to visit one of our schools. As director of education that was part of my job. We then continued our journey and crossed the border into the United States. We were on a small freeway with no shoulders, and it was pouring down rain. I pulled out and passed a semi truck, and then moved back into the right lane.

Suddenly, the driver's windshield wiper stopped working. I could not see where I was going. Looking out the passenger side I pulled off the freeway as far as I could without going in the ditch. It was a dangerous place to be especially in rainstorm where visibility was limited.

I got out to see if I could fix it, but it was hopeless. I had my mother with me since she was part of the vacation trip.

I said, "Mother, we better pray because I cannot fix this." We just finished praying and swish, this white pick-up truck pulled over just in front of us. The driver got out and came to my window.

"You must be an angel," I said.

He turned his head away and then turned back and asked, "Why do you say that?"

"Because we just finished praying, and here you are," was my amazed reply. I told him about the wiper.

He checked it out and said, "It will get you to your destination, but you must get a new wiper."

I was so grateful. I asked if he knew how far it was to the next town and he responded that he was not from the area and did not know.

He went to his truck and Mom and I looked away for a split second as I prepared to move back on the freeway. When I looked again, the truck was gone. We couldn't see it anywhere ahead of us. A few kilometers down the freeway it stopped raining, and we had sunshine the rest of the way to my son's place.

Think about this thing:

- God hears our prayers.

Notes:

CHANGE

"Wisdom hath builded her house, she hath hewn out her seven pillars" (Proverbs 9:1, KJV).

THE GRADUATION PROGRAM FORMAT NEEDED to be changed and updated, especially the Saturday evening program when the diplomas were handed out. We made the changes needed and of course not everyone was happy.

> *We made the changes needed and I received a phone call with a threat.*

I received a phone call with a threat that a certain wealthy person would not continue to contribute if the plan was implemented.

My response was, "Well, I am sorry to hear that, but we must do what is right for the school regardless of how it impacts the donations we receive. It is God's school, and He will provide."

The threat was probably not even credible, I don't really know. The point is don't allow yourself to be derailed if you have good logical reasons for doing things.

Think about these things:
- Change must be well thought through.
- Do what is right regardless of consequences.

Notes:

UNSKILLED VOYAGEUR

"What time I am afraid, I will trust in thee" (Psalm 56:3, KJV).

THE STUDENTS WERE EXCITED BECAUSE the entire school was going on a short canoe trip down a river not far away. I had never canoed and was not a good swimmer, so I was not exactly thrilled. However, I was assured that I would be with someone who was experienced.

The first half of the journey was quite enjoyable, but we had to make a change involving moving some people out of certain canoes and into other canoes. I was given two young boys to help me complete the rest of the canoe ride. Well, they were about as skilled as I was. Fortunately, the river was not deep, so the chance of drowning was pretty much nil, and we all had lifejackets.

The rest of the journey we slalomed across the river banging into the riverbank on one side of the river and then going back across to the other bank where we banged into that side. It was hilarious to say the least. We didn't give up, but eventually figured out the paddling idea, and we finally reached our destination.

Think on these things:
- Remain calm.
- Keep a sense of humour.
- We are not always prepared for what life throws at us.

A MOST UNLIKELY MAESTRO

"Praise ye the Lord: for *it is* good to sing praises unto our God; for *it is* pleasant; *and* praise is comely" (Psalm 147:1, KJV).

OUR CHURCH DECIDED TO DO an outreach program for our community. We had a choir and a small orchestra. It was a wonderful project for our church, and this was a new adventure to share this in a public venue.

I was part of the choir. However, we needed a maestro to keep everything together. I was chosen, not for my musical ability, but there was no one else. My basic elementary music training with very rudimentary conducting fell way short of what was needed. Stress!

Somehow God realized our need and we got through this crisis. Many people erroneously thought I knew what I was doing! The Great Musician had sent His angel.

Think on these things:
- God will supply our need.
- Allow God to use you.

NEEDING FUEL

"Now unto him that is able to do exceeding abundantly above all that we ask or think, according to the power that worketh in us" (Ephesians 3:20, KJV).

"I was hungry and you fed me" (Matthew 25:35, KJV).

I DON'T REMEMBER WHAT CLASS it was, but I am guessing it was Bible or math because those were always the two first morning classes.

One little cherub shared that he was hungry because he did not have breakfast. A few others shared the same experience. This had never happened in all my years of teaching, so I believed this was a real need.

I didn't respond to the hungry angel, but unknown to the students, I called my husband to bring bread, milk, cereal, peanut butter, and jam, and drop it off in the staff lunchroom. When I knew the supplies had arrived, I took the whole class to the staff room for breakfast.

They really enjoyed a good breakfast. One of the students sweetly commented, "Mrs. Fortney, now we know for sure that you love us."

Think on these things:

- Empty tummy, empty brain.
- Feed the hungry.

Notes

SPECIAL CLOTHES

"Naked, and ye clothed me" (Matthew 25:36, KJV).

MY BLIND STUDENT AND HIS sister loved to come to church and Sabbath School, but they had no church clothes. Their home life was less that adequate to say the least.

I purchased some church outfits and kept them at my house. Their Grandma would drop them off at our house on Sabbath morning; they would change into their Sabbath clothes and off to church we would go. After church, they would change their clothes and hang them up for next Sabbath and Grandma would pick them up and take them home. They loved it as they felt they looked like all the other children in their Sabbath clothes.

Think on these things:
- Go the extra mile.
- We need to show Jesus' love by our actions.

Notes:

CHOSEN AS PRINCIPAL

"For the body is not one member, but many"
(1 Corinthians 12:14, KJV).

I WAS THE VICE PRINCIPAL of a K-12 academy, and our principal was retiring. I was on the Personnel Committee to choose a new principal. The committee members wanted to put my name on the short list. I declined. There were many names who I considered much more qualified for the job.

Privately, I had prayed, "Lord if you want me to do this you will have to make this very clear." We continued to meet for several weeks going through many names. Nothing was falling into place. We had considered thirty-five names, and we were down to the last five names.

Again, the committee members asked, "Please, can we put your name on the list?"

I agreed but stipulated that my name had to be the last one on the list and that every other name had to be considered before mine. God made it very clear. It came down to my name as the name of the best possible candidate.

The committee members said, "We really believe God wants you to do this."

I believe He did. He was with me all the way throughout the time I was leading the team. It was four wonderful years, and then I took time off to complete my master's degree in leadership and administration. God is so amazing!

Think on these things:
- God has a plan.
- He will equip you to do the job.
- Surrender to God's will.

"It was the will of God that Adam and Eve should not know evil" (Education, p.23).

TOUGH CONSTITUENCY MEETING

"Fear thou not; for I *am* with thee: be not dismayed; for I *am* thy God: I will strengthen thee; yea, I will help thee; yea, I will uphold thee with the right hand of my righteousness" (Isaiah 41:10, KJV).

CONSTITUENCY MEETINGS CAN BE INTERESTING, and of course there are always those who have axes to grind. At this particular meeting there were those who focused on the problems. I assured them that, of course, there were challenges. No matter what organization, school or church, there are always problems to solve. That admission took the wind out of their sails, and we were able to move on with solutions rather than focusing on the problems.

The school board chair gave a little speech about the fact that they couldn't find an experienced principal, so they had to grow their own, referring to me of course, because I had been the vice principal for a couple of years.

When it was time for me as the new principal to speak, I referred to the board chair's comment with this response: "The board chair mentioned that you had to grow your own principal. Well, being a farm girl, I know what it takes to grow a good crop, so how about we have a lot more sunshine and a lot less fertilizer." The place erupted with laughter, and it set a new tone for the meeting and for the school year.

Think on these things:

- A sense of humour can relieve tension.
- Offense is better than defence.
- Wisely agree with your adversary.

INTIMIDATION

"Then Peter opened *his* mouth, and said, 'Of a truth I perceive that God is no respecter of persons' " (Acts 10:34, KJV).

A NEW SCHOOL BOARD CHAIRPERSON was chosen and one day he came to my office to connect with me in my capacity as the principal of the school. He wanted to discuss how we might cooperate together to move forward with the school vision. He made a statement that was interesting.

He said, "My wife is concerned about our relationship." I thought, well, surely this has nothing to do with getting romantically involved. He was quite a bit my senior. Granted, his position in society carried a fairly heavy influence.

I questioned, "Is she concerned that you might intimidate me?"

"Yes," he responded.

"Well," I said, "Let's take care of this right now. You don't intimidate me." He knew I meant what I said.

Think on these things:
- Leaders cannot allow intimidation.
- We are all the same at the foot of the cross.
- Respect all people.

Notes:

INVISIBLE VISITORS

"The angel of the Lord encamps all around those who fear Him, and delivers them" (Psalm 34:7, NKJV).

I WAS TEACHING GRADES ONE to four in a multi-grade classroom. We were learning about angels so I thought a little physical illustration would help the students to understand the reality of guardian angels. Before the students arrived, I placed a chair beside each student's desk. When they saw the chairs, they were excited because we were going to have visitors.

"When will the visitors get here?" they asked.

"They are already here, and they have taken their seats, but you cannot see them." I explained that I was speaking about their guardian angels. It was interesting, to say the least, to see the look on their faces as they thought about the reality of the angels actually being present, but unseen.

Think on these things:

- God is real.
- Angels are real.
- God's word is true.

Notes:

HOLY SPIRIT TIME OUT

"Train up a child in the way he should go: and when he is old, he will not depart from it" (Proverbs 22:6, KJV).

THERE WERE TIMES THAT AS teachers we would ask, "Is it the full of the moon?" The students seemed to be agitated and disgruntled and not being kind to each other. It was like the wrong spirit was in the room.

At these times, I would stop whatever we were doing and make a call to prayer. We would all kneel, and I would pray and give opportunity to any of the students who may want to pray. We would ask for God's presence to be with us and if there were any evil angels that slipped into our classroom that they would be dismissed.

I always marveled at the results of our prayers. There was such a sweet peace and a calmness, and we were able to continue with our work.

Think on these things:

- Our adversary is like a roaring lion.
- The Lion of Judah is our protector.
- God hears our prayers.
- Children need to see active faith.

Notes:

TWO CORRECT ANSWERS

"Have I not written to thee excellent things in counsels and knowledge?" (Proverbs 22:20, KJV).

ONE OF MY PRECIOUS LITTLE first graders put an "L" as the beginning letter that represented the beginning sound for the picture of a boat. I was puzzled, and so the next day when I returned his book, I asked him why the "L"?

> *One first grader put an "L" as the beginning letter for the picture of a boat.*

"It is the "Love Boat," my little one replied.

"Well, that would be correct then," I assured him. I chuckled as I thought about his choice. Sometimes, there are two correct answers.

Think on these things:

- Ask questions.
- Keep an open mind.

Notes:

RAW TRUTH

"Not everyone that saith unto me, 'Lord, Lord', shall enter into the kingdom of heaven; but he that doeth the will of my Father which is in heaven" (Matthew 7:21, KJV).

SADLY, THERE ARE MANY IN positions of leadership that may not have converted hearts. There was shocking behavior taking place behind the scenes that was unknown to others, but was known to God. I experienced a situation where there was a mean spirit, there was gossip, and there was an undermining of the school leadership.

The devil never slumbers. However, neither does our God, and He is much more able in every situation. God took care of this situation in a way that was very striking. There was such a fallout and brokenness in the lives of these dear people that it was astonishing.

Think on these things:
- Do your job.
- Vengeance belongs to God.
- God is omniscient.

HOLD THE LINE

"And the Lord shall make thee the head, and not the tail; and thou shalt be above only, and thou shalt not be beneath; if that thou hearken unto the commandments of the Lord thy God, which I command thee this day, to observe and to do *them*" (Deuteronomy 28:13, KJV).

OUR SCHOOLS WILL ONLY BE the head if the leadership lives each day with Jesus. You cannot take the staff and students to higher ground if you as a leader are living in the swamp, and your relationship with Jesus is non-existent.

There were many evenings that the lights were still on in my office, and on one of those evenings a colleague was also working. I had a question regarding a certain invoice and so I simply crossed the hallway and entered his office. He immediately clicked off his computer screen. To make a long story short, this person was watching things that God's people shouldn't be watching. There was sin in the camp.

This situation was revealed as the Bible tells us that God sees all things. We may hide them from men, but never from God.

Think on these things:

- Achan brought trouble to the entire nation of Israel.
- Be compassionate, but never affirming to those who fall into sin.

Notes:

DISCERNMENT

"Even a child is known by his doings, whether his work *be* pure, and whether *it be* right" (Proverbs 20:11, KJV).

ONE STUDENT WHO STOOD HEAD and shoulders above many was a little Catholic girl who really enjoyed the Bible classes. One day she shared with me that she and her mom had been reading the Bible and they were finding that the Bible did not support the teachings of her church.

"You know," she said, "there are a lot of smart Catholics out there. Why can't they see that something is wrong?"

It is at these moments I am once again reminded and convinced that our schools are evangelistic centers. God help us not to lose our mission.

Think on these things:

- The Word of God is powerful.
- God's people are everywhere.

Notes:

TEST RESULTS

"When pride comes, then comes disgrace, but with humility comes wisdom" (Proverbs 11:2, NIV).

SEVERAL YEARS AFTER I RETIRED, I received a message from one of the parents whose child I had tested for reading. I had totally forgotten this situation. Apparently, whatever I said when sharing the results of the test, made her think that this child was not going to do well in life. With what she understood me to say at the time, I told her she should have boxed my ears! I simply apologized and was so glad to hear that her son was a very successful businessman. The right words can make such a difference and apparently, I didn't get it right.

Think on these things:
- Perception is someone's reality.
- Word choice is so important.

Notes:

DRUGS IN SCHOOL

"For there is no respect of persons with God"
(Romans 2:11, KJV).

ONE OF MY MOST PRECIOUS students was caught selling drugs at school. His parents had been killed in a car accident and he had been adopted by a very good family. He had need of nothing materially as his adopted parents were wealthy and they treated him well, with love and kindness.

We were faced with a tough decision, but we had to take this to the board with a recommendation for expulsion. It was a sad day for our staff. The board was unanimous in their decision to expel this student. Time confirmed this was the right decision as this young man was able to transfer to another academy, where the right person was able to take him under his wing and exert a real positive influence in the young man's life.

Think on these things:
- Rules are for everyone.
- Love and kindness have a positive influence.

Notes:

A PRAYER ROOM

"One Lord, one faith, one baptism, One God and Father of all, who is above all, and through all, and in you all"
(Ephesians 4:5-6, KJV).

A FAMILY FROM A CERTAIN religious group wanted to enroll their children in our school. After enrolling, a few days later, they asked for a prayer room to pray to their god. It was explained to them that this was a Seventh-day Adventist School and the only religion promoted here was the Word of God as understood by the Seventh-day Adventist Church. Prayer and worship were part of the program, and all students were to be present at special services. In addition, prayer and worship were part of the daily program within the classrooms and all students were expected to participate in these activities.

"What you pray quietly in your heart is up to you," we told them.

This was not enough accommodation for them, so they chose to go elsewhere.

Think on these things:

- Love all people.
- There is one God.

"To every teacher is given the sacred privilege of representing Christ. And as teachers strive to do this, they may cherish the reassuring conviction that the Saviour is close beside them, giving them words to speak for Him, pointing out ways in which they can show forth His excellence" (Testimonies for the Church vol. 7, p. 274).

INTERFERENCE

"But Jesus knew their thoughts, and said to them: 'Every kingdom divided against itself is brought to desolation, and every city or house divided against itself will not stand' " (Matthew 12:25, NKJV).

WE HAD TO DISCIPLINE A certain young lady for participating in behavior that was not acceptable. She was not happy about this, and her family went to the school board chairperson where they found sympathy and support.

As the principal, I rebuked the chairperson for taking a stand against administration without checking to see why or what the situation was regarding the discipline. He was interfering with out any knowledge of the facts. We met with the educational superintendent, and the chairperson was educated on due process. Bless his heart, he took it with humility.

Think on these things:
- Following due process saves embarrassment and stress.
- Gather the facts first.

Notes:

LIGHTS ON THE MOUNTAIN

"Neither do men light a candle, and put it under a bushel, but on a candlestick; and it giveth light unto all that are in the house" (Matthew 5:15, KJV).

WE WERE ON A SCHOOL campout at the foot of some very steep mountains. There was a trail to the top of one particular mountain and it was a favorite hiking challenge for many over the years. Two of our high school boys decided to hike this trail at night for their own reason.

The lights they chose to shine were not exactly ones that would fit the song, "This Little Light of Mine." However, their lights shone, and the school's security guard could see very clearly the situation. These boys had no idea that lighted cigarettes can be seen at night for a distance of five hundred meters. This attribute of light was the reason that during WW II sailors were not allowed to smoke on the decks of their ships at night.

Unfortunately, for the two boys, their parents were called to come and pick them up and they missed out on the campout.

Think on these things:
- Be kind, but consistent.
- Where there's smoke, there could be fire.

Notes:

KNOW YOUR GIFT

"And God hath set some in the church, first apostles, secondarily prophets, thirdly teachers, after that, miracles, then gifts of healings, helps, governments, diversities of tongues" (1 Corinthians 12:28, KJV).

ONE OF THE FINEST GENTLEMEN I have ever known in my life joined our staff as a teacher of the ninth grade students. He was a successful army officer, very intelligent, and very pleasant. However, he really struggled with classroom management.

> *He was a successful army officer. However, he really struggled with classroom management.*

When we reached the time of rehiring staff for the next school year, he came to my office. He simply shared with me that he recognized that in spite of the help he had received, he was not successful in managing the challenges of behavior in the classroom. He would not be seeking continued employment. He recognized this was not one of his gifts. Like I stated, he was very intelligent. We would miss him, but he was correct in his assessment of his skills, and I admired his wisdom and courage.

Think on these things:
- Follow God's plan for your life.
- Be honest with yourself.

Notes:

SANTA ANA WINDS

"Confess *your* trespasses to one another, and pray for one another, that you may be healed. The effective, fervent prayer of a righteous man avails much" (James 5:16, NKJV).

ONE MORNING I GOT AN urgent call from the band teacher, who was not a member of our church, stating that he could not come in for band class because he needed to stay by the phone. (This was in the days before it was common for everyone to have a cell phone.) His daughter's house was right in the path of a fire, and she might have to evacuate at any minute. I assured him that his needing to stay where he could be reached was not a problem and that I would have the entire school pray about this situation. We had a special prayer for God to save his daughter's house.

It wasn't long before the band teacher called me again. He was amazed at the miracle that had just happened. The wind had changed directions and blew the fire back over the mountains. His daughter's house was saved. He was so impressed he shared this story with the congregation the next time the band performed in church.

Think on these things:
- God answers prayer.
- He is the master of the wind.

EARLY MORNING VISITOR

"Wine *is* a mocker, strong drink *is* raging: and whosoever is deceived thereby is not wise" (Proverbs 20:1, KJV).

OFTEN, I WOULD GO TO school early in the morning to prepare for the day. One particular morning I was reading the Bible story regarding Saul and the witch of Endor. It is a somewhat creepy story, but the Bible tells it like it is (was).

I heard the outside door open, and soon I saw two huge, gnarled hands gripping the side of one of the swinging doors. Then this older, tall male person entered into my space.

I was somewhat alarmed, but I managed to keep my composure, knowing that there was a way of immediate escape, if need be. I also could see that he was obviously very drunk and was having a hard time standing. I wasn't too afraid.

"Good morning, Sir. How may I help you?" I politely asked him.

"Is the pastor here?" he asked.

"Just have a seat and I will call him for you," I responded.

I left the room and entered the church, called the pastor who lived close by. Bless his heart, he came immediately even though it was six a.m.

After this incident I was careful to lock the outside door even though our school was located in a small community.

Think on these things:
- Locked doors are a safety measure.
- Plan B is a must.

WEAKNESS

"And Moses said unto the Lord, O my Lord, I am not eloquent, neither heretofore, nor since thou hast spoken unto thy servant: but I am slow of speech, and of a slow tongue" (Exodus 4:10, KJV).

PUBLIC SPEAKING IN STRESSFUL SITUATIONS was not a strength of mine, particularly at certain types of meetings. I was a much better listener. I was somewhat terrified at the first board meeting after I was chosen to be the principal of a K-12 school. I must tell you that I didn't impress anyone at that meeting. It was like I froze and couldn't think of what to say or how to say it.

After the meeting as the school board chair and I sat in my office, she said, "You'll have to do better than that."

I already knew that I really flunked out as a principal at that meeting. I believe that God allowed that to happen so that I would always realize that I had to depend on Him. The Lord gave me courage, and from then on, I was able to communicate my thoughts clearly even in difficult situations.

"Humble me so I can do Your will," was my prayer. I did not apply for the position, but God had made it very clear that He was calling me to the position.

Think on these things:
- When God calls you, He equips you.
- Failure can lead to great success.

> **To every worker I would say: Go forth in humble faith, and the Lord will go with you. But watch unto prayer. This is the science of your labor. The power is of God. Work in dependence upon Him, remembering that you are laborers together with Him. He is your Helper. Your strength is from Him. He will be your wisdom, your righteousness, your sanctification, your redemption. (Testimonies for the Church, vol. 7, p. 272)**

STRANGE FEAR

"Trust in the Lord with all your heart, And lean not on your own understanding" (Proverbs 3:5, KJV).

TEACHER'S CONVENTION WAS TO BE held on a cruise ship. Wow! That sounded great, but I wondered how I would fare as I often got sick simply by riding in the back seat of a car.

Anyway, it was a few hours drive to the airport so off we went. I say "we" because my husband was coming with me. As we got nearer to the airport, I got this real fear of going on the cruise.

"I can't cop out on this trip," I moaned. "I am supposed to be the fearless leader of the teachers."

My children said, "Mom, we don't think you should go."

I found this very troubling, and I finally said, "Ok, I am going to call the president and let him know I have this strong impression not to go on this cruise."

The president reassured me. "Listen, you just don't worry about it. Get some rest and relax, we will manage without you." It really was quite strange. We drove back home feeling like we really let everyone down, yet we felt that we made the right decision.

Within a day or two after we returned home our friend Laurence died. He had started attending our church and had recently taken part in the communion service. He had been diagnosed with cancer and had finally succumbed to the disease.

His family was at a loss as to what to do about a funeral. My husband asked if they would like to have his funeral in our church. He shared the story of Laurence's attendance at our church over the past several months. They were so relieved. We called our Adventist pastor. We organized our little congregation to provide a lunch for the funeral attendees after the service.

Laurence's sister said, "Because of my brother's lifestyle I had no hope of seeing him again, but after what you have shared with me, I believe I will see him again."

Had we not been home this would never have happened. God knew we had a more important work to do.

Think on these things:
- God directs our lives in different ways.
- Sometimes things don't make sense at the moment.

Notes:

HYPOCRITE IN UNIFORM

"But be ye doers of the word, and not hearers only, deceiving your own selves" (James 1:22, KJV).

I INVITED THE POLICE DEPARTMENT school liaison to come and speak to the grade five and six students about drugs and alcohol. He gave a great presentation with a lot of visual samples and statistics. He then had a "question and answer" session.

"Do you drink alcohol?" one of the boys asked.

I could see there was a reluctance on the part of the officer to answer the question, but then it came, "Yes, I do."

I am sure he couldn't help but see the shock and confusion on the faces of the students. I am also sure he was aware that hypocrite would be an appropriate word to describe him at that moment.

The young student who asked the question looked around at his peers with an expression of triumph. There were no more questions.

Think on this thing:

- Walk the talk.

Notes:

URGENT VERSUS IMPORTANT

"Beloved, if God so loved us, we ought also to love one another" (1 John 4:11, KJV).

A SWEET CHILD WITH ALCOHOL syndrome struggled with many issues. One of the issues was the fact that math was not easy for her. On one particular day, because she didn't understand a certain concept, she did not get her homework completed.

I took a little time to help her, and as I was up at the board taking her through some examples, she called out, "Mrs. Fortney, could you just forget about that right now and come and give me a hug?"

Her greatest need at that moment was not understanding how to divide fractions, but to know that she was loved.

Think on these things:
- Identify the greatest need.
- Be willing to listen.

Notes:

CONCLUSION

TO GOD BE THE GLORY! This is my testimony and some of my experiences over the years working with Him, our great and awesome God, Creator, and our wonderful Savior. I pray that you will be encouraged whatever you may be teaching, or if you are in administration. Always remember that there is no problem He cannot solve.

Be strong in the Lord.

"Work as if you were working for your life to save the children from being drowned in the polluting, corrupting influences of the world" (Testimonies for the Church vol. 6, p. 199).

BIBLIOGRAPHY

White, Ellen G. *Education.* Mountain View, CA: Pacific Press Publishing Association, 1903.

———. *Testimonies for the Church, Volume 6.* Mountain View, CA: Pacific Press Publishing Association, 1900.

———. *Testimonies for the Church, Volume 7.* Mountain View, CA: Pacific Press Publishing Association, 1902.

TEACH Services, Inc.
P U B L I S H I N G

We invite you to view the complete
selection of titles we publish at:
www.TEACHServices.com

We encourage you to write us
with your thoughts about this,
or any other book we publish at:
info@TEACHServices.com

TEACH Services' titles may be purchased in
bulk quantities for educational, fund-raising,
business, or promotional use.
bulksales@TEACHServices.com

Finally, if you are interested in seeing
your own book in print, please contact us at:
publishing@TEACHServices.com
We are happy to review your manuscript at no charge.

www.ingramcontent.com/pod-product-compliance
Lightning Source LLC
Chambersburg PA
CBHW042133160426

43199CB00021B/2894